HEY RE

Did you k
you're holding more than just a book?

Included are two special features from Javier Vásquez Jr.
He is an actor and the author of this book.

1

A Personal Video Message
Just for you!

Scan here to access the video message:

2

An Audio Narration
Read along with Javier.

Scan here to access the read-along:

BOOKS+MORE

Expanding the joy of reading
through multi-media innovation.

BERRY POWELL PRESS

Discover more books at www.berrypowellpress.com.

JJ's Audition Adventure
Copyright © 2024 by Javier Vázquez Jr. and Ekaterina Soyuznova

This is a work of fiction. Names, characters, organizations, places, events, and incidents are either the products of the author's imagination or are used fictitiously. Any resemblance to actual persons, living or dead, or actual events is purely coincidental. Printed in the United States of America.

All rights reserved. No part of this publication in print or in electronic format may be reproduced, stored in a retrieval system, or transmitted in any form or by any means, electronic, mechanical, photocopying, recording, or otherwise without the prior written permission of the publisher except for use of quotations in a book review.

First hardback edition July 2024
Cover Design by Ekaterina Soyuznova and Kay McConnaughey
Published by Berry Powell Press
Glendora, CA

ISBN: 978-1-957321-17-2 (hardback)
ISBN: 978-1-957321-16-5 (paperback)
Library of Congress Control Number: 2024906778

PRAISE FOR
JJ's AUDITION ADVENTURE

"I love this fun, informative, entertaining, and accurate depiction of life as an actor. Javier has mapped out the passion and love we feel as artists and shared it in a way anyone, including children, can understand and embrace. Bravo!"

—Terri J. Vaughn, Actress, Director, Producer

"If you know a kid who thrives in the spotlight, this book is an absolute must! It's an awesome, clever tool to help children develop their love for entertaining into a practical and potentially lifelong career."

—Jason Lockhart, President of Atlanta Models & Talent and Head of TV/Film

"*JJ's Audition Adventure* is like a treasure chest full of wisdom and wonder, perfect for any young dreamer aspiring to shine on stage or screen. With every turn of the page, you'll smile, tear up, and cheer as JJ bravely faces the ups and downs of the world of auditioning and being an actor.

It's a story that's as honest as it is entertaining, teaching valuable lessons about perseverance and determination along the way. Get ready for an adventure that's bursting with heart and boundless imagination!"

— Regina Ting Chen, Actress

"*JJ's Audition Adventure* is a thoughtfully written picture book filled with lively illustrations that inspire young actors to pursue their dreams, while reminding them to have fun along the way."

—Denise Santos, Mom, Actress, and Founder of Latinas in Media Atlanta

"This story is fantastic! Javier does an excellent job with the storyline, the hopefulness, and the excitement the characters feel on every page. The illustrations are absolutely beautiful and engaging for kids. It is an excellent book for any classroom. It teaches kids the value of perseverance and hard work."

—Ana Hortman, Teacher of the Year, Gainesville City Schools

"This story is a master class in how to support and encourage someone who aspires to act. I wanted to read and reread it for its message of positivity, perseverance, and family teamwork."

—Amy Hamilton, Retired Educator and Librarian

"*JJ's Audition Adventure* is an artfully illustrated children's book of a young, relatable character's hopes, dreams, and desires. JJ will connect with the journeys and hopes of young readers who flip the pages of this heartwarming story of what's possible for a dreamer."

— Dr. William Campbell, Middle School Principal, Minneapolis Public School District

For my nieces and nephews. You can do it! I believe in you!

—Javier "Tio JJ"

To kids who dream big.

—Ekaterina

JJ's Audition Adventure

Javier Vázquez Jr.
Illustrated by Ekaterina Soyuznova

BERRY POWELL PRESS

This is JJ. He's in the third grade. When he's not at school, playing soccer, or hanging out with friends, one of his favorite things to do is put on a show!

Once, he and his little sister Mimi dressed up as astronauts and pretended they were flying a rocket to the moon.

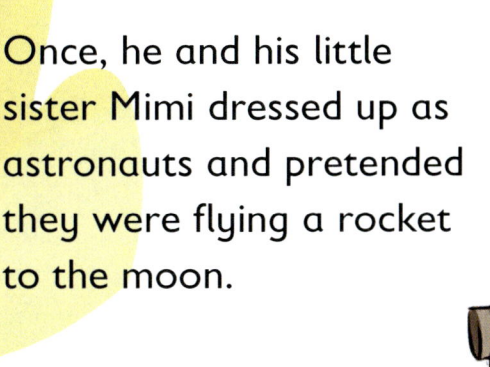

Another time, he used wooden spoons, pots, and pans as instruments to put on a live concert for his parents.

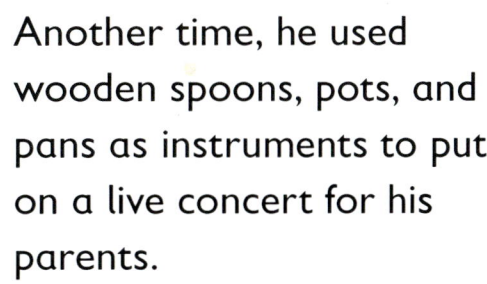

Even at school, he makes his teachers and friends laugh with his funny faces.

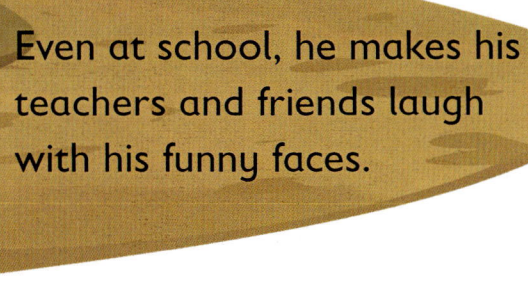

One night, JJ and his family were snuggled up on the couch to watch their favorite TV show. JJ leaned back between his mom and dad, with his little sister Mimi asleep on their dad's lap.

"Remember, I said there would be a surprise in this episode," said Dad. Mom and Dad smiled at each other as though they were hiding a secret.

"Okay, Dad," said JJ. Suddenly, a voice everyone recognized came through the TV. JJ's eyes widened as he turned to see someone familiar on the screen.

"It's him, it's him!" yelled JJ.

Mom was so excited she almost dropped her popcorn. Mimi woke up, rubbing her eyes and looking around.

"What's going on?" Mimi asked.

JJ pointed to the TV screen. "Look, It's Tio Rolando!" he exclaimed.

All of their eyes were focused on the TV. With a big, friendly smile, there on the screen was Uncle Rolando, or "Tio," as JJ called him, acting in the family's favorite show!

The living room instantly burst with happiness as they watched him play the role of a brave cowboy.

Mimi shouted, "Go back! Go back, Dad! I want to see the whole thing!"

Dad said, "Don't worry, sweetie. We'll show you." He reached for the remote.

"Call your Tio," said Mom to JJ, "I'm sure he'd love to hear from you."

"Hey, Tio! We just saw you on TV! I can't believe it! It was so cool! Dad said there would be a surprise, but I didn't think I would see you on our favorite show!"

On the other end of the video call, Tio Rolando smiled from ear to ear. "Thanks, JJ. I hope you liked it."

"We loved it!" JJ exclaimed. "How did you get on the show?!" JJ ran into the other room to listen better.

"Well," Tio Rolando explained, "My job is being an actor! That means I get to play different characters on TV, commercials, movies, radio, and sometimes even plays."

"Wow! I can't believe my uncle is famous! I want to be an actor, just like you," JJ said with confidence.

"Whoa, whoa, whoa! Slow down!" Tio said, with a kind voice, "You're already an actor. Remember the school play you did last year? You made us all very proud."

JJ responded, "Yes, but I want to be on TV and commercials and movies like you!"

"Are you sure?" asked Tio. "It's a lot of work, you know."

"Oh yeah!" JJ responded confidently. "My dad says I'm a hard worker. Can you teach me?"

Tio Rolando smiled. "Of course. I'm **on set** this week…"

"On set?" JJ interrupted.

"Yes, I'm on set for a movie. Look!" Tio turned his camera to show where he was. Through the cell phone, JJ could see bright lights, giant cameras, big machines, and lots of people moving things back and forth. JJ was instantly fascinated.

"I'll be back home next week," said Tio. "We can get started then."

"YES!" exclaimed JJ. "I can't wait."

"The director is calling me—she's in charge here. I have to go, but I'll see you next week. Bye, JJ. I love you."

"Bye, Tio. Love you too!" said JJ.

JJ ran back into the living room. "Hey, guess what? Tio is coming over to teach me how to be an actor!" he said dramatically, with his hands in the air.

"You're weird. Can we watch Tio on TV again?" said Mimi.

JJ laughed. "Yeah, baby sister. Let's go!"

When Tio Rolando arrived the following week, everyone was so happy to see him. JJ and Mimi jumped into his strong arms as he spun them around.

"Hey, baby sister!" Tio said to JJ's mom as he gave her a hug.

"Hey, movie star," she replied. "Did you bring me anything from Hollywood?"

"Girl, I wasn't in Hollywood. I was in Florida!" he responded playfully. "But I did bring you this." Tio handed JJ's mom a box of delicious pastelitos, fruit-filled pastries covered in powdered sugar.

"Ooh," she squealed. "Those would go great with coffee. Let's go to the kitchen."

As the family sat down for pastelitos, JJ asked, "So when will I get to be on TV?"

"Let's take it one step at a time, kiddo," said Tio. "First, you need a **headshot**. A headshot is a really nice picture of yourself. Lucky for you, your dad is a photographer."

"Great idea!" said Mom. "I'll call him now and ask him to bring his camera home from work."

"Next," said Tio, "you have to get an **audition**."

Mimi looked up. With powdered sugar all over her face, she asked, "What's an audition?"

Tio Rolando smiled, grabbed a napkin, and wiped her face as he explained, "Well, an audition is like trying out for a sport, but instead of... say... a basketball team, it's for a team making a movie."

Mimi nodded and replied, "Ohhhh."

"So how do I get an audition?" asked JJ nervously.

Tio smiled and leaned in as if he was sharing a big secret. "There are many steps, but I'll try my best to explain.

Whenever someone wants to make a movie, they usually hire a person called a **casting director.** That person will find actors and invite them to audition for the acting roles.

There are a bunch of websites casting directors use to find actors. I'll show you my favorite one.

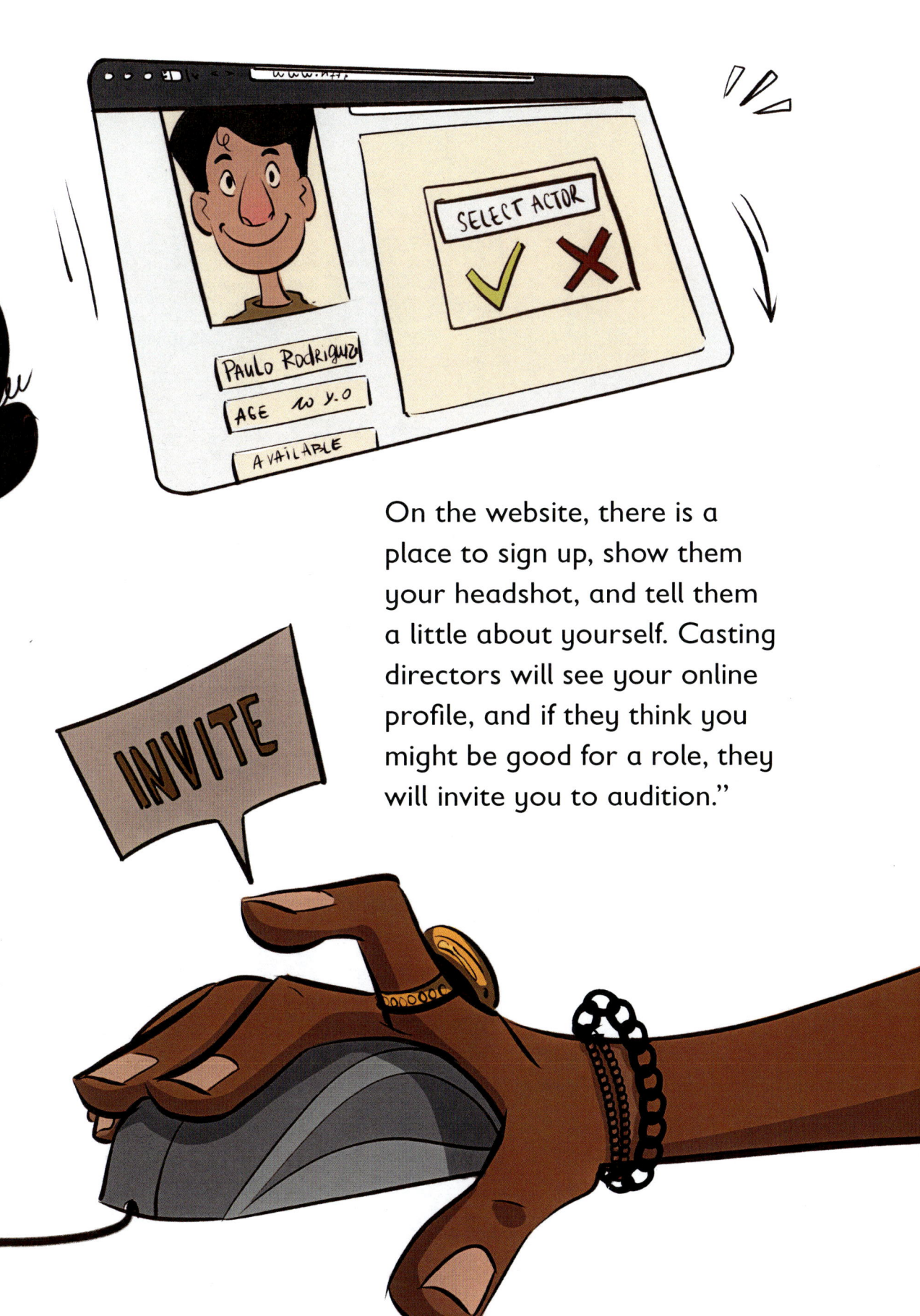

On the website, there is a place to sign up, show them your headshot, and tell them a little about yourself. Casting directors will see your online profile, and if they think you might be good for a role, they will invite you to audition."

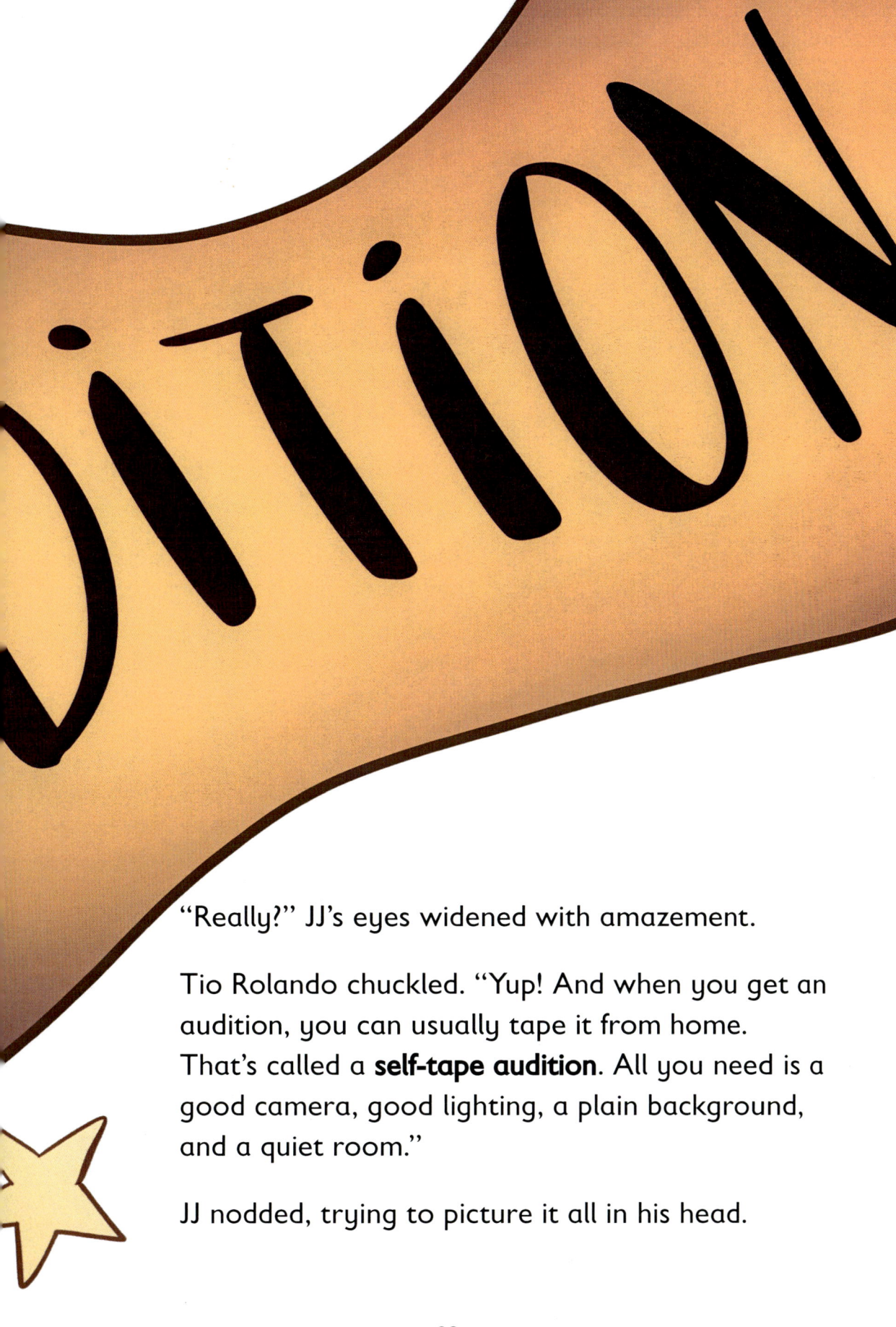

"Really?" JJ's eyes widened with amazement.

Tio Rolando chuckled. "Yup! And when you get an audition, you can usually tape it from home. That's called a **self-tape audition**. All you need is a good camera, good lighting, a plain background, and a quiet room."

JJ nodded, trying to picture it all in his head.

"Hey, sis," Tio said to JJ's mom, "do you still have that tripod to hold up the camera or cell phone while recording? We need it to make sure the camera stays steady during the self-tape."

Mom replied, "Yes, we do, but just say the word, and we'll buy a new one, big brother. When it comes to shopping, and to help JJ, I am always ready."

Tio laughed. "Well, that's great because we need a backdrop and good lighting!"

Mimi pointed to the ceiling lamp. "We already have lights up there."

Their uncle shook his head gently. "No, baby girl, those are too high. We need a light that shines right on JJ's face."

Mimi's eyes widened. "Oooooh," she exclaimed.

"Look! I found a few backdrops online," said Mom, holding up her phone. "Which one should we buy?"

"Wow! That was fast," said Tio.

Mimi quickly voiced her opinion, "The one with the cats!"

"No way! I like camouflage," JJ said.

But Tio suggested, "Actually, that solid blue one is best. You want something simple that doesn't distract from your performance, JJ."

JJ trusted his uncle's opinion and nodded in agreement.

The next day, Dad used his camera to take JJ's headshot. Tio helped them pick the very best picture, and they uploaded it to the acting website. They also filled in some basic information about JJ, like his age, height, and hobbies.

JJ's mom and Tio looked through roles on the website and found one that would be perfect for JJ. It was for a short film that needed a third-grade kid who could play soccer. They sent them JJ's new headshot and mom's email address and crossed their fingers.

A few days later, Mom's phone beeped. She looked at an email on her phone and smiled at JJ, saying, "JJ, come look at this! The casting director responded and invited you to audition for the role! Look, she sent your lines—those are the words you'll say in your audition. It also says your audition tape is due Friday."

"Really?" said JJ. "What do we do first?"

"Okay!" she said. "This is how Tio Rolando explained it. Step 1: You memorize your lines. Step 2: We record your self-tape audition. Step 3: We email your tape to the casting director. Step 4: If you are selected, they will contact us with the good news. Step 5: If you get the role, your scene starts filming next month!"

He was excited, but he also felt a little worried. Deep inside, he wondered if he could really do it. He was used to acting in front of his family and friends, but this was for a real film project. Not only that, but he only had a few days to prepare!

He was determined to try his best. He worked hard, practicing his lines. He stayed away from TV and video games. He even read his lines out loud in the car while going to and from soccer practice, using every moment to become the best actor he could be.

Finally, the moment arrived. It was time for JJ to record his self-tape audition with the help of his family. He stood in front of the camera, a bit jittery.

"Just breathe, mijo," said Mom, using the comforting Spanish word for "my son." JJ took a deep breath.

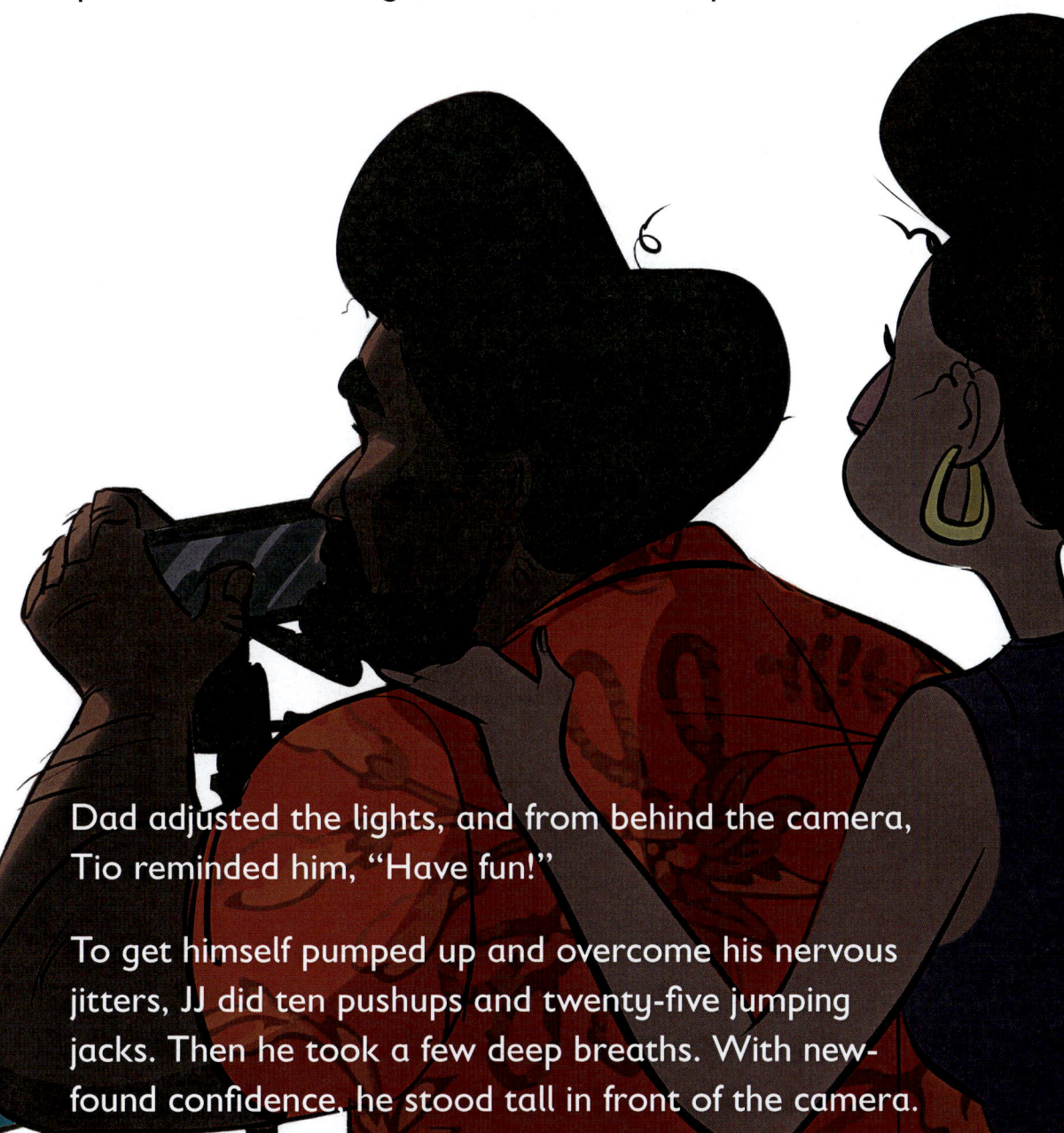

Dad adjusted the lights, and from behind the camera, Tio reminded him, "Have fun!"

To get himself pumped up and overcome his nervous jitters, JJ did ten pushups and twenty-five jumping jacks. Then he took a few deep breaths. With new-found confidence, he stood tall in front of the camera.

"**Let it rip!**" Tio shouted, and JJ started acting.

JJ had to pretend he was in a stadium full of people. In his mind, he imagined them all around him cheering. He bounced the soccer ball on his knee and then said his lines as they were written on the paper. His mom then read the lines for the other character in the scene, speaking in a quiet voice so JJ's voice would stand out.

Everything was going smoothly until Mimi started chasing their cat right through the middle of the room.

JJ yelled, "Everybody, quiet!"

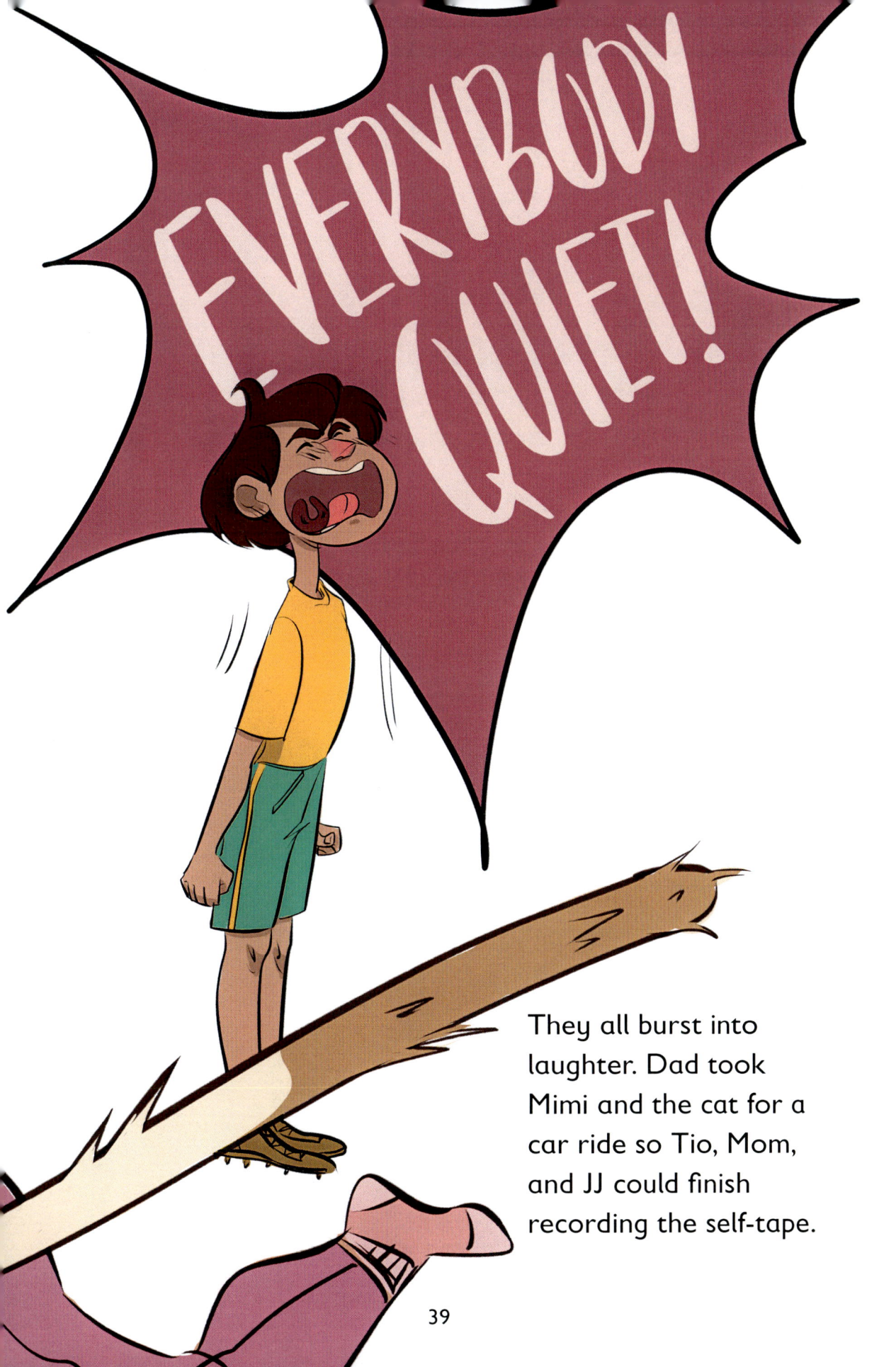

They all burst into laughter. Dad took Mimi and the cat for a car ride so Tio, Mom, and JJ could finish recording the self-tape.

They recorded the scene several times, and JJ felt more confident every time. Finally, Tio said, "I think we've got it. That was great, JJ!" and he turned off the camera.

JJ couldn't help but feel proud of himself and of his family who helped him. "Thanks for helping me! You both did great too!"

They looked at each other and smiled. "Aw, thank you, JJ," his mom replied, wrapping him in a hug. "Don't tell your dad, but you get your skills from our side of the family." They all laughed.

Later that evening, JJ couldn't contain his excitement as he peeked over his mom's shoulder. She made sure to follow all the directions the casting director had given her. The video was ready. The computer made a "whoosh" sound as Mom sent his audition to the casting director. The job was done. Now, all they could do was wait.

JJ turned to his uncle and asked, "What's next?"

Tio explained, "Well, now the casting director will receive all the audition tapes and pick the actor she thinks is best for this role!"

Curious, JJ asked, "How many people will audition?"

"Lots of talented kids will also be trying out for the role. So, there's no promise you'll get it. And if you don't get the role, chances are the casting director won't even call you to give you the bad news."

JJ couldn't help but wonder about all those other auditions flowing toward the casting director's computer. He realized every one of those kids also wanted to be in the show.

"Wow!" said JJ, surprised. "So, if I don't get the role, they won't even call me to tell me what I can do better next time?"

"No, they won't," said Tio. "Listen, JJ. The most important thing is to have fun and be proud that you had the chance to audition at all. Not everybody gets a chance to audition."

"That's true, Tio, but I just know I'll get it," said JJ.

"I hope so," said Tio. "You did what you could. The rest is out of your hands. Just be a kid, play, go to school, and enjoy your life."

A couple of weeks passed, and it felt like forever. JJ's impatience grew and grew. He said to himself, "I learned my lines, set up my lights and backdrop, recorded my audition, sent it in, and still haven't heard if I got the role. I'm so tired of waiting!"

While Dad was busy doing the dishes, JJ asked, "Any news yet?"

"Not yet. You must be patient," said Dad

As Mom sat at the kitchen table paying bills, JJ blurted out, "Any emails?" Mom shook her head.

When playing with his sister Mimi, all he could think about was the audition, and he asked, "Has Mom mentioned anything about my audition?" Mimi looked at him with her big, innocent eyes, clearly confused.

JJ stared into the cat's eyes. "Blink twice if you think I'm going to get the role." The cat just walked away.

Frustrated, JJ threw his arms in the sky and yelled, "WHAT IS TAKING SO LONG?!"

That Saturday, the family went to the park. The adults looked at each other. Dad nodded and said to Mimi, "Sweetie, how about we go on the swings so Mami and Tio can talk to JJ?" Without thinking twice, Mimi darted toward the swings.

JJ sensed something was up. He asked, "Am I in trouble?"

Tio reassured him, "No, buddy. You're not in trouble, but there is something I want to talk to you about. Do you remember when I told you that they probably wouldn't call you if you didn't get the role?" JJ nodded. "Well, I just wanted to let you know that I think they picked someone else for the role."

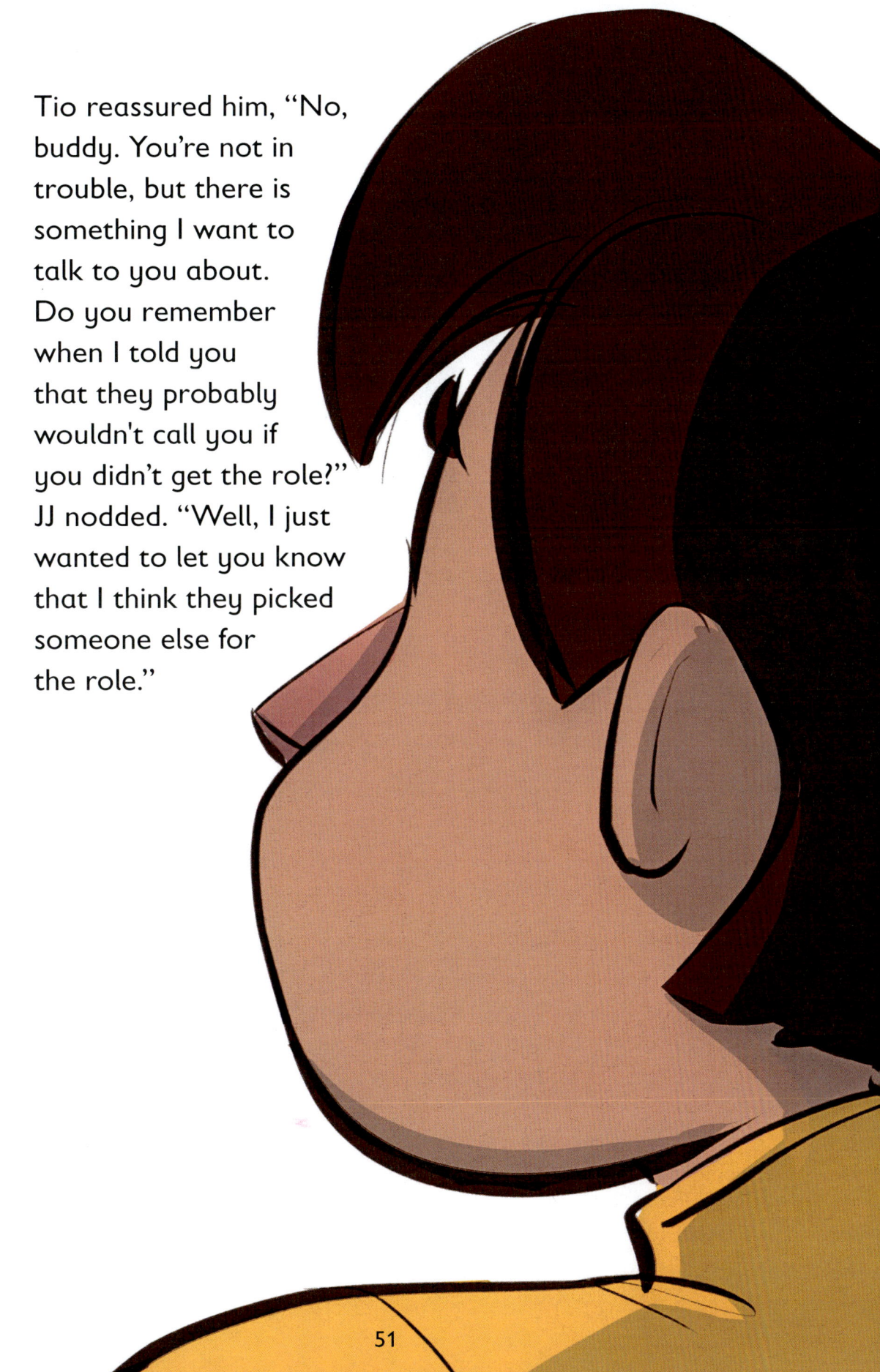

"What?" said JJ with confusion. "How do you know? Did they call you?"

"No, mijo," said Mom. "But the website said filming starts on Monday—"

"So, there's still a chance?" JJ interrupted.

Tio shook his head. "They would have called you by now. I'm so sorry."

JJ was in shock for a moment, and then tears filled his eyes as the disappointment set in. Red-faced, he turned and ran off to be alone.

Tio Rolando knew exactly how JJ felt. He said, "I'll talk to him." Mom stood there with a concerned look, knowing how hard JJ had worked and how much he wanted this role.

JJ found a quiet spot by a nearby pond and sat with his head on his knees, crying. Tio sat in the grass beside him.

JJ looked up, and tears rolled down his cheeks. "Why didn't they like me?" he asked, his voice quiet and shaky. "I tried so hard, and I really thought I was going to get it."

"I've been an actor for many years, and I've had hundreds of auditions," Tio said warmly. He put his arm around JJ, and JJ leaned into Tio's shoulder. "But most of the time, I don't get the role, and I never find out why. In fact, one year early in my career, I wasn't chosen for a single acting role."

"Really?" It seemed to JJ that Tio always knew what to do. He couldn't imagine his uncle not getting a role.

"Yup. That's just part of being an actor. There are lots of times you don't get the part even if you did a great job. It just means someone else was a better fit," Tio confirmed.

"How do you do it? How do you keep trying when you do your best and still don't get the role?" JJ wondered aloud.

Tio looked at the water and pointed to a duck gliding gracefully on the surface. "Look at that duck over there," he said. "He goes underwater, but he doesn't get wet. His feathers don't absorb the water. They repel it, and it rolls right off. That's how I treat my auditions. If I don't get it, I just let it go. Like water off a duck's back. If I book the role, I will be grateful.

"I didn't become an actor because it's easy. I became an actor because I love it. I love making people laugh and smile. I love telling stories and for people to see those stories come to life. Sometimes they pick me, sometimes they don't. But I never give up!"

JJ listened intently. "But what if I'm not good enough at being an actor?"

"You are good enough," Tio encouraged JJ. "Everyone can do amazing things in life, but we have to take it one step at a time. And you took a big step with this audition. I want you to think about how much you've learned!"

JJ took a moment to think, and a small smile appeared on his face. "I guess I have learned a lot," he admitted. "I learned about cameras, lights, and backdrops!"

Tio nodded proudly. "Yes, you have. You tried something new, got a headshot, memorized your lines, turned in a self-tape audition, and then waited patiently for the news. For a young actor, that is a big deal."

"Well, I wasn't that patient, but you're right," JJ admitted, his smile growing wider.

"And now it's time for another lesson," Tio Rolando said with a twinkle in his eye.

Curious, JJ asked, "What's that?"

Tio leaned in and shared his wisdom. "Forgetting about this audition and getting ready for the next one with pride. That is if you still want to be an actor. Is this something you really want to do?"

Immediately, JJ responded, "I do!"

"Is this something you really love, even if it means being disappointed sometimes?"

"Yes! I want to be an actor," JJ replied.

"Then say it like you mean it!" Tio smiled widely.

JJ jumped to his feet, raised his arms, and shouted, "I want to be an actor!"

Tio celebrated with JJ. "That's what I'm talking about!" he said, and he gave him a high five.

The rest of the family joined them on the grass,

"Why are you guys yelling?" Mimi asked.

JJ giggled. "We're not yelling," he said, "I just want the whole family to know that I can't wait for my next audition."

"After JJ gets his next audition, can we get some ice cream?" said Mimi as she sat beside her brother. The whole family laughed.

"What's so funny?" Mimi asked, puzzled.

Dad crossed his arms and said, "How about we get ice cream first?"

"Yes!" said JJ. "But wait! Are we celebrating that I did NOT get the role?"

"No," said Dad as he put his arm around JJ's shoulder. "We are celebrating that you were brave, and you did your best. I'm proud of you, mijo."

JJ smiled, nodding up at his dad. "In that case, I'll have two scoops of ice cream! And I'm sitting next to Tio!" said JJ.

"I want to sit next to Tio!" Mimi pouted.

"You can both sit next to Tio," said Mom with a smile.

Piling into the car, the family drove off to celebrate **JJ's AUDITION ADVENTURE.**

The End!

GLOSSARY

- **BACKDROP:** A plain cloth or surface that goes behind you in an audition so nothing in the background distracts from your performance

- **CASTING DIRECTOR:** The person who watches auditions and chooses the actors for a play, movie, commercial, or TV show

- **LINES:** The words an actor says in their audition or performance

- **BOOK A ROLE:** To be chosen for a part in a play, movie, commercial, or TV show

- **LIGHTING:** Special lights are sometimes purchased for self-tape auditions to make the actor more visible

- **"LET IT RIP":** To give it your all or do your best

- **"EVERYBODY QUIET!":** A phrase film makers say when they want everyone to be quiet

- **AUDITION:** A short performance (on video or in-person) to show your acting or singing skills

- **TRIPOD:** A stand to hold a cellphone or camera, so it doesn't shake while recording or taking pictures

- **HEADSHOT:** A special picture of you that focuses on your face to help casting directors remember you

- **"ON SET":** The place where the movie, commercial, or TV show is being filmed; there's usually a stage surrounded by lights, cameras, and other people working on the show

- **SELF-TAPE AUDITION:** A video audition that you make yourself; you act out your part, record it on a camera or phone, and send it to the people who choose the actors

LETTER TO YOUNG READERS

Dear Reader,

Thank you for reading my book about JJ turning in his first self-tape audition! As an actor, I have seen many creative children like JJ do excellent jobs in movies, on television shows, and in commercials. I usually play their dad, and I am amazed by how hard-working and responsible these young actors are. My children followed in my footsteps as entertainers. I have been there to guide them and am so proud of what they have accomplished so far.

    I hope you found inspiration in JJ's exploration of the exciting world of acting. He had many obstacles to overcome, but like Tio Rolando, he never gave up. My goal is to help guide you as well if acting is something you are interested in.

    If you want to be an actor someday, talk to your family to see what's possible. You could join an acting class, try out for a part at school, or put on a show in your living room! Your parents can visit my website (www.ExploreTheSpark.com) for more ideas on how to get started.

    Whatever your passion, whether acting, drawing, painting, singing, dancing, or playing an instrument, remember that you can achieve your dreams with hard work and the support of those who care about you. Just like JJ, keep reading, dreaming, and believing in yourself.

    Thank you again for reading my book. I hope to share more stories with you soon!

Best wishes,
Javier

LETTER TO PARENTS

Dear Parent,

If you're reading this book, you may have a budding artist or performer on your hands! Whether your child wants to be in the spotlight or just wants to step out of their comfort zone, this is an exciting journey to go on with them.

Alongside the excitement, so many questions come with being a parent in this industry. How do I get my kid an audition? How can I help them improve their skills? How do I make sure my child is always safe on set? I've been there. Besides my acting career, my three kids have followed in my footsteps, growing their careers in the performing arts. That said, I'd love to share some insights on the most important things for parents to know.

First, I want to speak to the idea of "exploring the spark." As parents, we can see when our kid has a unique interest, talent, or passion budding inside them. Whether acting becomes a career or not, it can be an excellent way for kids to use their imagination, practice bravery, and find their voice. If your young artist is interested in the performing arts, there are so many ways you can support them. Community theatre, courses, camps, and coaches—both online and in person—are often just a click away. I always encourage parents and kids to explore the spark and see where it goes!

As you venture into the entertainment industry, I want to emphasize that vigilance is essential. Please thoroughly research agencies, casting calls, and opportunities that come your way. If you have to pay to play, you should probably walk away. You can look at my website for more information on what to look out for. Verify the authenticity of organizations and individuals involved, and never hesitate to seek references or ask questions. This approach empowers you to make informed decisions prioritizing your child's interests.

Equally vital is safeguarding your child's physical and emotional health. Acting is fulfilling yet demanding. It's crucial to help them balance their passion with sufficient rest, education, socialization, and leisure time. Open communication and a supportive home environment will help them navigate the highs and lows they'll encounter. My three children continue learning how to manage this highly competitive field best. Yet it has been so fulfilling, and they express themselves at newer heights daily. Film is an incredible outlet for creativity when well-monitored and balanced.

I created Explore the Spark to help kids develop their passion for the performing arts. Please check out the website for additional resources, and reach out if you have any questions. While there, you can also sign up for the newsletter, where I will continue to share valuable insight into the world of TV and film acting. I'd be thrilled to embark on this journey together and witness the growth of your talented young actor.

Warmest regards,
Javier Vázquez Jr.

www.ExploreTheSpark.com

ACKNOWLEDGMENTS

I am overwhelmed with gratitude for all the people who have poured into my life and career. There are so many I would like to thank.

First, I would like to thank my high school sweetheart, Karla, who has stood by my side all these years and for whom my heart beats stronger every day. I am the person I am because you are by my side. My children, Jeilianne, Enrique, and Caleb, have been my ever-present readers. Your creativity and talent never cease to amaze me, and there is nothing you can't do. Thank you for all the late nights and last-minute auditions. I cannot do this without you. To my parents, stepparents, godparents, aunts, uncles, and teachers: thank you for the strength, love, and belief you instilled in me.

Ekaterina Soyuznova, thank you for partnering on this project with me from day one when this book was just a dream. You brought these characters to life. We did it!

Amy Hamilton, you encouraged me every step of the way. Your insight and belief in me provided the strength I needed to push through. You are such a blessing to me and my family.

The heart of this book is tied to all those who have mentored me. I'm grateful for Rolando Gómez (Tio's namesake), fellow author Maria Pérez-Gómez, and my professors Gerry Trentham and Drew Kahn. Thank you for playing a foundational role in helping me explore the creative spark early on. To Jason Lockhart and the Atlanta Models & Talent team, thank you for lifting me on your shoulders. I'm grateful to the vibrant creative community in Atlanta for its unwavering support of local talent, my hometown of Buffalo, NY (Go Bills!), and my adopted hometown of Gainesville, GA (Go Big Red!).

Lastly, this book would not have been possible without the amazing Carmen Berry, Abigail Dengler, and the entire team at Berry Powell Press, including Kay, Valeri, Marianne, and Carolyn. Your feedback and guidance have made me a better and more thoughtful writer.

—Javier Vázquez Jr.

Creating this book has been a dream come true! Just like JJ, I couldn't have done it without those who helped me along the way.

Of course, I want to thank my family for supporting the journey. Big thank you to Anna Egorova for believing in me. Mary Kuper, thank you for sharing my passions and guiding with love and compassion. Matt Maloney, thank you for creating an environment to explore different avenues of an art career and teaching healthy life habits. Vinod Krishnan, thank you for your wisdom and for not being afraid of my planner. Thank you, Manohar Kumar, for welcoming me on my first set and giving me the opportunity to meet with my fellow collaborator on this book, Javier, whom I thank for inspiring and motivating me to create something as special as this. To our team at Berry Powell Press, especially Carmen and Abby, thank you for taking a leap of faith in our creation.

Lastly, I would like to thank me (Grandma said it's important!) and my puppy for keeping me active after long hours spent creating this book and projects to come.

—Ekaterina Soyuznova

ABOUT THE AUTHOR

Born and raised in Buffalo, NY, Javier is the oldest of nine. He pursued a career in education, working for The Buffalo Public Schools and the Gainesville City School systems. Javier holds elementary, middle grades, and high school teaching certifications in several states. In 2012, he booked his first movie role in an independent feature film. After securing an agent, he landed roles on network television and major motion pictures such as Venom, starring Tom Hardy, and Clint Eastwood's The Mule with Bradley Cooper and Michael Pena. He has had dozens of speaking roles on television and film and countless appearances in commercials, voiceover, and print work. Represented by Atlanta Models & Talent, Javier continues building his resume in acting, writing, and production. Beyond writing and acting, Javier is a storyteller on a mission to inspire, uplift, and celebrate the wonder of childhood through the performing arts.

Learn more at www.ExploreTheSpark.com.

ABOUT THE ILLUSTRATOR

Ekaterina Soyuznova is a Russian illustrator specializing in character design and storyboard creation. At seventeen, she ventured to the UK to get an illustration degree from UAL (University of the Arts London). From there, she set her sights on the US, where she found her true calling as a character and story artist while studying at SCAD (Savannah College of Art and Design). From books to webcomics to film sets, she's worked with companies such as Malka Media, THT, Catholic Stories, IBX, Ingenuity Studios, Creative Mammals, and more. In addition to her work on JJ's Audition Adventure, she has an ongoing webcomic called Monster Pet. She currently lives in Moscow, where she loves reading comics and watching Doctor Who with her dog, Mira.

Learn more at www.EkaterinaSoyuznova.com.

NOTE FROM THE PUBLISHER

We at Berry Powell Press believe that every child is born with unique gifts and talents to be developed and expressed. To encourage children and their parents to cultivate these gifts, we are delighted to publish *JJ's Audition Adventure*, written by Javier Vázquez Jr. and illustrated by Ekaterina Soyuznova.

Our goal as a publisher is to create books that open previously closed doors or reveal doors kids never realized were available to them. Many talented kids never get to explore their creativity through acting because they, or their parents, don't know how. We are proud of how this book gives each young reader an uncle, or "Tio," to show them that it's not as scary or impossible as they might think and that they have more options than they ever dreamed possible.

This book also embodies our emphasis on inclusion, rooted in Javier's own story. Growing up, Javier had a talent for acting. Still, as a Puerto Rican kid whose family was not wealthy, he never knew the entertainment industry was an option for him until later in life. As a working actor, Javier's goal is to show children they have options in today's entertainment industry, regardless of their race, ethnicity, class, gender, religion, ability, or any other factor. We are thrilled to imagine the diverse generation of young creatives who will grow up with this book as a model for exploring what lights them up inside.

We at Berry Powell Press are committed to cultivating authors and their life-changing messages through building a collaborative, creative community of authors and publishing professionals. If you have a book rumbling around inside of you that needs to be written and released, please visit our website at www.berrypowellpress.com. Contact us, and we can explore if we might be a fit.

Carmen Renee Berry
New York Times bestselling author
Founder of Berry Powell Press
wwwberrypowellpress.com

Berry Powell Press is a hybrid publishing house that publishes authors with transformational perspectives on timely personal and societal challenges. Our authors are provided in-depth mentorship and collaborative assistance to create life-changing books and to build book-based businesses that can impact the largest audience possible. We publish fiction and non-fiction for adults and children.

Made in United States
North Haven, CT
22 January 2025

64837578R00049